P9-EDR-054

Patricia
Hampl

Woman
Before an
Aquarium

University of Pittsburgh Press

Published by the University of Pittsburgh Press, Pittsburgh, Pa. 15260
Feffer and Simons, Inc., London
Manufactured in the United States of America

Library of Congress Cataloging in Publication Data

Hampl, Patricia
  Woman before an aquarium.

  (Pitt poetry series)
  I. Title
PS3558.A4575W6   811'.5'4   78-4115
ISBN 0-8229-3378-0
ISBN 0-8229-5294-7 pbk.

The author would like to thank the National Endowment for the Arts for a grant awarded in 1976, during which time some of these poems were written.

Some of these poems first appeared in *Amazon Quarterly, Anthology of Minnesota Poems by County, Aphra, Dacotah Territory, Ironwood, Momentum,* and *25 Minnesota Poets* (vols. 1 and 2).

"Charlotte's Web," "Fire Engine," and "Wild Rose" were first published in *American Poetry Review.*

A selection from "Questions of Travel" from *Questions of Travel* by Elizabeth Bishop, copyright 1956 by Elizabeth Bishop, is reprinted with the permission of Farrar, Straus & Giroux, Inc. This poem appeared originally in *The New Yorker.*

*The publication of this book is supported by a grant
from the National Endowment for the Arts
in Washington, D.C., a Federal agency.*

For Jim Moore

Together we'll look at the world . . .
— Osip Mandelstam, "The Goldfinch"

CONTENTS

Call Me Home

MOTHER-DAUGHTER DANCE

Because it is late
because we fought today
because it was hot
and heat is an excuse
to be alone,
I sit in this chair stuffed
with old sun, leftover heat.

Our fight. The subject as always was history.
You made me look over my shoulder.
Mother was back there, speaking
to us in epilepsy, that language
she learned on her own,
the one we encouraged her to use
at the dinner table.
In my mind, I fell down, writhing,
trying to make history repeat itself,
burning with translations of guilt
for the men in the family.
Father forced a yellow pencil
between Mother's teeth, like a rose:
you die if you swallow your tongue.

All afternoon you yelled at me
as I slithered nearer to her.
We were doing the mother-daughter sweat dance,
salt dance, sexy Spanish rose dance.
You were yelling from the English language,
that fringed island I swim toward at night.
"The pencil," you were screaming in your language,
"Take the pencil from her mouth.
Write it down,
write your message down."

TRES RICHES HEURES

1

A house stands
in the middle of the prairie.
Inside a woman sits
with a sewing basket
piled with dreams
which are not wishes.
These are actual dreams,
full of spinsters
who cover their new pale shoes
carefully with kleenex,
where inappropriate women sit
before things called hearths.
Do they know where they are?
They keep saying,
"This is a museum. Be afraid."

2

A time
when all the parts of a life
were balanced like animals
with their perfect tails.
My father's greenhouse:

> *Go play in the palm house*
> *till I call you for dinner.*

Wedding palms, rented for weddings,
were also funeral palms,
rented for funerals.
In the dark tubs, cats
and field rabbits came
to give birth to their wet, unfinished babies.

Here, in the midst of her most coiled fantasy,
the most private story of jungle life,
the little girl was also thinking happily:

> *Call me home,*
> *call me home for dinner.*

3

I sit in a pine-board house,
nervous,
my lip gnawed ragged:
something of a nightmare
simply in sitting.
But the present moment is
spread out before me,
if only I could grasp it.
Spread like an illuminated manuscript
bright with tendrils of memory and future.

This balancing tail
reaches the hours
I must return to,
back to the possibility
of saying

> *Mother, Father,*
> *you did not stop me.*

CHARLOTTE'S WEB

for my Mother

I am sitting on the dock.
My mother is reading to me.
It is the summer
I killed leeches,
curling them up with salt.
It is the summer
I almost drowned,
the summer I first stepped out of my body,
my hand touching a bolt of wool
in the Hudson's Bay store
while my brother buys a china teacup.
I cannot tell where my hand stops
and the fabric begins.
From across the room I am touching
the pale English downs
of the cup's landscape.

My mother is next to me,
holding the fabric she will buy.
I have entered other objects.
I want to ask if she knows
what I mean.
But suddenly the current snaps off,
I am not imprinted on the cup my brother is holding.
I left my skin and entered
several yards of red wool,
but I am back.
I am inside.
I can be removed from the Hudson's Bay store
without pain.

We are on the dock.
My mother reads
Charlotte's Web and stops
when I cry.
"Darling! Don't cry!"
"Keep reading, keep reading," I sob.
The voice starts up again
dry as hazelnuts,
slow voice that doesn't try to get away,
voice that does what I want,
softly bringing the story I love,
voice with more ocean than the ocean that laps near us,
voice, woman who cries for the death of a spider too.
Mother! We are on the dock,
rising and falling with fiction.

"CLAIR DE LUNE"

I play the notes,
familiar old water-song,
dray horse of grade school recitals
leading children to water,
to that Mediterranean
of music, French, engulfed
like a cathedral, a rose window.

Joy of the hands, each finger
a body, ten musicians
performing a chamber concert
for the perfect audience of two ears
alone in my empty hall.

And now the moon rises
over the water
as it was meant to
so many years ago,
my small head
setting slowly in the hard wood
of my father's piano.

THE CAR IN THE PICTURE

My father is sitting on the grass
in a sleeveless cotton-ribbed undershirt.
He is looking off somewhere
to something we will never know about.
It must be night, it must be summer.
I am laughing. Chokecherry lips, tiny peg teeth.
My hand is touching his shoulder,
a daughter's doll hand,
hot ingot of joy impressing
itself into his life.
Behind us, that black car,
a case of beer on the running board,
a Chevy, "from before the war," as my father says.
From before me,
from the August nights when the men sat
together on the grass, watching
the green frill of the algae
lighten on the lake and become ghostly.
When someone would break
the silence to say,
You buy a Studebaker,
you buy a Rambler,
you'll *never* be sorry.

WOODEN STEAMER CASE

My great-grandmother
could live in this trunk.
her clean bones piled
like linen hemstitched
fine as milk teeth.

Her life
is also in the trunk,
children placed side by side there:
the stillborn, those who grew to manhood.
Her closed Sunday parlor,
shrunken like a head,
put in with the keyhole intact.

Her son, my dead grandfather,
goes in with his concertina,
the bust of Masaryk,
and five new pennies to give
for somersaults.

My father is young
and Uncle Frank is still
a prizefighter, makes $35
a week which is more
than anybody else, and alive.

The trunk takes us back
(the dead and the rest of us)
to Ellis Island,
to the ocean which is gray
and three weeks long,
takes us to Hamburg, to a train,
to Prague; then in wooden shoes
to Kutná Hora where

we are born
into a European dream.
We air the family bones,
set up house speaking Czech.
All the furniture has flowers
painted on it. We are peasants.
Then we must eat. We go outside,
we brazenly shoot pheasant,
because we want to,
in the noble's estate.

BIRTHDAY DURING A LENTEN SERVICE

A churchful of bent knees, an altar,
something gold, a candle burning.
God was not as stern as we'd been told.
This was the secret: He was shining and He had a hand.

Lent was purple, full of Fridays.
We made the Stations of the Cross, 14 death steps.
We sang *Oh Star, Oh Star of the Sea.*
My birthday rose in a blizzard on a Friday.
The nave of the church was filled with shipwrecks,
singing in the white storm.
A piano was somewhere in my brain, unrepentant,
hammering its green felt hammers, making
                    a shoe of music for dancing.
A piano, a harp
            laid on its side in a rosewood box,
a body of clean music in its shiny coffin,
Lazarus of the hands: the music would fly up
            on Sunday, a gold fork in the ear of the lily,
            a single footprint on the snow, a single son sacrificed.

I wanted a piano for my birthday, I want one now,
the moving men struggling up the stairs, through the blizzard,
bringing the music on its back, the awkward body of song,
the aching muscles, the frozen breath,
the snow they plunged through —
We knew prayer then, holiness, why we must dig
our fingers into the black and white life stretched before us.

FORTUNE-TELLERS

In the Portobello Road, a leathery woman
who carried a sprig of heather wrapped in tinfoil
said she could encourage me, for very little money.

The conductor on the stale train from Prague to Paris
grabbed my hand, instead of the ticket.
"This is good, this is excellent," he said
as we rattled past the hop fields.
All the way to Paris I studied
the huddled destinies curved in my palm.

The clairvoyant organist in a Wisconsin restaurant
stopped my mother as she went to her table.
"Why don't you write?" he asked her sternly.
He told her many other things about me,
but she won't reveal any of them. Just live,
she says. It will all happen.

Four Interiors and a Still Life

AN ARTIST DRAWS A PEACH

She wanted to depict man and woman
so she started with a snake.
It was green and flat as a ribbon.
It wasn't right, there was no curve
for a belly, no green under the green.
Even the huge apple had no far side to its red moon.

She was alone, she was willing to wait.
Then she saw the peach.
It held out its peach color.
She drew it, drew it out
of her body, it was the color
of the secret places of her body.
Was anyone else peach-colored
and bulging with another surface?

She incised the peach with a hairline stroke,
its pink split like a bivalve in water,
like her own buttocks; she could
breathe deeply again, the pink was released.
It folded its peach smoothly,
it bent toward its other side,
the flesh lit a candle under its skin.

Now she had teeth,
her tongue touched her own body.
I was so afraid, she said,
but the peach, it was the first
thing I really drew. I understood
its color. As for shape,
the shape was in the color.
My own body spoke
from its long shyness.

THE LETTER:
MARY CASSATT'S AQUATINT

It is over now, everything
she had to say is broken
in black upturned rows
like a plowed field in April.
She wears a blue figured dress,
the wallpaper is a skin of flowers behind her.
Love! Love! she has written. *A startled deer in summer!*
Her hieroglyphic thought is untransferable, like her flesh.
She sends it urgently to a woman far away.
Like everything that passes between them, this isn't words.
It is a white room hung with the smoky charcoal drawings
of the single perfect body they have in mind.
Friend! Comrade! A journey! she has written.
It is irrevocable, all her longing.
The white bird in her hand is her hand;
it sings desperately.
I want you to understand one thing.
But the language melts.
After betrayal, the emotions
have no declarative sentences,
only walls, the crumbled, vine-choked walls of friendship.
She sits in her blue dress, the wallpaper is
a sweating glass terrarium. A glass bowl
has cupped her life, the wall is papered
with endless green flowers, but it *is* a wall.
From beneath a blossoming branch she launches
a white letter in the slow afternoon.
It flies free. She shades her eyes to watch.
It goes in its own direction.

WOMAN BEFORE AN AQUARIUM

The goldfish ticks silently,
little finned gold watch
on its chain of water,
swaying over the rivulets of the brain,
over the hard rocks and spiney shells.

The world is round, distorted
the clerk said when I insisted
on a round fishbowl.
Now, like a Matisse woman,
I study my lesson slowly,
crushing a warm pinecone
in my hand, releasing
the resin, its memory of wild nights,
my Indian back crushing
the pine needles, the trapper
standing over me, his white-dead skin.

Fear of the crushing,
fear of the human smell.
A Matisse woman always wants
to be a mermaid,
her odalisque body
stretches pale and heavy
before her and the exotic wall hangings;
the only power of the woman:
to be untouchable.

But dressed, a simple Western face,
a schoolgirl's haircut, the plain desk
of ordinary work, she sits
crushing the pinecone of fear,
not knowing it is fear.
The paper before her is blank.

The aquarium sits like a lantern,
a green inner light, round
and green, a souvenir
from the underworld,
its gold residents opening and closing
their wordless mouths.

I am on the shore of the room,
glinting inside
with the flicker of water,
heart ticking with the message
of biology to a kindred species.
The mermaid — not the enchantress,
but the mermaid of double life —
sits on the rock, combing
the golden strands of human hair,
thinking as always
of swimming.

ELEGY AND DRAWINGS

for Annie Hayes

Your plant drawings watch over my desk
now that I've returned from my long absence,
unsteady, holding the thinnest pen I've ever used,
like the one that sketched these roots and water veins,
whose ink stream reminds me
of the quivering calligraphy of the Declaration of Independence.
It is wonderful to hold this independence, to watch it write
words I may come to love,
to see, when I glance up, your own black strokes.
You don't draw plants for beauty
but to remind us how awkward growth is.
I see the Swedish ivy contains a story about death,
the tender accuracy of withering.
How do you know these things?
One empty cup in the corner, the serenity of jasmine tea,
the sudden absence in that corner of any life or striving.
Did you know how glad we would be
and not know why?
Today I am planning a funeral
for an old woman nobody loved anymore
because she had lived too long.
Her only wish toward the end:
"I hope I don't go in winter
so it'll be a trouble."
But it is February and a great blizzard is predicted.
A tiny, withered woman, born in a covered wagon,
saw the fresh prairie flowers,
rode across them, crushing them as plants
crush the air they reach through to grow.
Going West was simply reaching toward the sun.
She loved Dakota; she loved an empty space.
Will you understand tomorrow when I shred

21

your black and white flowers and scatter them
on the grave of an unmourned woman?
I will place your word there too:
iris,
plain-lettered, double-sided word,
the Chinese idea of flower,
cut and definitely dying.
And for one who will not see again,
iris again,
bluish memento of vision.

JAN BRUEGHEL'S BOUQUET

Shoe-polish black background,
and his flowers strike
the hour of full bloom;
extinction begins in the next shadow.
The open tulips show their black rods
and the cornmeal of their stamens.
Garden iris, grained papers
too watery to write on,
and peonies the color of sliced ham.
An open fan of white breath,
ecru details of gypsophelia.
The green stems have been painted
into disappearance, they have entered
the shining black wall.
He has made primary color a memory:
tulip, iris, the descriptions
of red and blue for a blind man
touching his own face.
The petals curl; they are limp, bent
away from resilience and pumped blood.
Two insects dangle from their own silk,
two marionettes of leftover sex touching
the completely black petal
dead center in his composition:
the entire alphabet of the iris.
The way he says black,
then black again, black, black.
Then, listen! everyone in every century! —
Black, it is black, black
at the center of the picture,
at the edges, at the heart of the flower,
at the crux of the known world:

I say it is shining,
I say it is black and shining,
I say it and my name is Brueghel.
I am saying good-bye
from century to century.

Narodni Galerie, Prague
May 1977

North Shore

WHO WE WILL LOVE

for Phebe Hanson

The old man from the next cabin is inspecting the rocks.
He has a jeweler's eyepiece, and the picnic table is covered
with Precambrian chunks of Lake Superior.
This shoreline looks like the Maine coast,
the oceanic breakers, the boulders jutting out
to meet the water like the north Atlantic shelf.
This old man is our best example of New England.
He is tall, the lean puritan body bends with stern attention
over the marvelous multiplicity of God's plainness,
the repetitive rocks, the limitless plate of unbroken water,
the unbudging glacial history of the boulders
that speaks of the slowness of violent change.
He has attended to all of this for forty summers.
He is so beautiful, we all want to fall in love
with stoical ministers who are charred with doubt,
with watchmakers who repair fine old timepieces,
with farmers who wake up early to split oak logs
and stack them in piles for winter.
We'll fall in love with anyone who
takes his time, who looks, who agrees
to keep looking for forty years at least,
who believes in the truth of the microscope,
whose head gets whiter and frailer every summer,
whose response to the wind-blown opening
of the wild rose is, "Yes, correct."
He must believe in the rigorous clock of the seasons,
he must be able to count.
Beyond that, his time is his own.
The spiderwebs hoisted between the starry asters
that shiver with cold dew,
the sleek timothy grass and the hair of the buffalo grass,
the raspberry bushes, the gooseberries

27

in their thorny lives, the silky black and white skunk
who turned shyly, who did not want to fight,
the young seagull whose feathers are still mottled
like the egg he came from,
the stones, the stones, the stones,
the lapping fresh water, the soft, unfired
bowl that holds the water:
we will love
who loves all this.

ICE AGE

The plain cabin, its single room
set on the edge of the lake
like a shell, a pale stone,
a stone among stones.
I am here, warm;
the solid ice-block
of last night's dream is melting,
soaking into my brain.
The ice age has been here a long time.
At night cold rushes into me
like a granular tide over pebbles.
I am a shore, the flowing is like seasons.
Everything rushes toward winter,
toward ice, toward meaning.
I sleep under quilts
but all night I rub my hands
over that glittery, transparent block.
I gnaw the edge of the dream;
I want to digest mystery.
But ice lives a rigid life,
laying its plank
across my body at night.
How many days I never wake at all,
curled in the ice-field
like a lost mountaineer
who realizes at last
it is the snow
not the mountain
he wanted.

WILD ROSE

for Carol Conroy and Chris Cinque

The metal lake is silent today.
The tips of the waves aren't gleaming
in rows like English horns.
No sun, no flare of pastel at the horizon.
The Minnesota rose on the shore folds around its center
in five exhausted skins of pink.
The lovely body of dew that usually burns
away in the morning light
is streaking the petals with thin blue veins.
Nothing wakes up — not the sun;
not the quivering water in its dream
of cloudiness and bent tin;
not the insect who, yesterday, chewed
this green serrated leaf; not the boy
who called out that he could skip stones;
not even the rose is alert to the gray morning,
to the blue bruises that must have come in the night,
                                        with the dampness.

SUNBATH

Someone fat, who knows she's fat,
on a rock, red skirt, white blouse,
two white arms of sun in the sun.
All along this shore bright dots
who work all year are on vacation.

The lake has become the sky, the sky
the water. The blue world is upside down
with relaxed muscles. The pink leg
stretches. The year unclenches a fist
of weeks in a hidden pocket.
Hands on rocks, opened, petaled like the wild rose.

Relax now, no work; be the snake
of slothfulness, flick the tail of leisure;
an orange cat the color of wood purrs
in your hair.

THE WAVE

The man is Chinese, his wife
is what I am, flat white cheeks,
putty-colored corduroy, knowledge
of being less beautiful than he.
Their little girl is flinging sticks
into the campfire, although
there is no campfire, and it is
a gray morning, 10 o'clock.
The sky is falling
into the lake in a stream of fog.
The man and his wife sit very close,
together on the driftwood log.
His head is bent toward hers
as if the waves must not interrupt her,
as if he will listen to her forever.
Even their daughter doesn't come between them.
She builds her imaginary fire,
she collects stones that are small eggs.
Standing toe to toe with the crashing wave,
her small stalk turned away from them,
toward the gray water and friendlessness,
toward some other way of speaking, she screams
into the flying wave. Her red
plastic jacket, the black zero
of her open mouth, the one high note.
Then she turns away from the water,
back toward her mother and father, sees
yes, they are still there, still
listening to each other,
still bent over the murmur,
still holding the world together.
She goes back to the stinging wave.

COLOR'S APPROACH

The sun has just come out of its envelope,
the thin gash between lake and sky.
It is spreading across the water,
it has reached the burned leaves of the gooseberry
and turned the fog on the rose hips
to droplets of clear water.
The broad grassy slope is becoming vivid.
Soon the sun will touch my tennis shoes.
I have a bouquet to take home:
late lavender asters and goldenrod,
a branch of mountain ash
with its heavy fall of red berries,
another red branch of shore dogwood
whose white berries are pellets of dough.
I touch my toes ten times
and feel the stretched rubber of my leg muscles.
I sit on the picnic table that nobody uses,
and stare at the advancing sun
and the chrome of the lake.
I wait for the post office to open,
for Doris to say, "Do I ever
have something for *you* today."
My friends will arrive with their intricate love affairs.
There will be cold white wine
and the tarry smell of roasted corn.
The clouds will send out their endless displays of form
across the blue September sky.
The air will be winter,
the iron-ore boats will fall silently
over the rim of the horizon
like faith, hope, and charity into certain disaster.
The cars on 61, full of hunters,

will hurl themselves toward Canada and the animals.
The Cross River Falls will rush on, sounding
strangely like an office air-conditioner.
All of this happens every day,
only more so, more so.
The aster becomes precise,
the yellow frill of its center makes more sense
as it fades and the pollen smears.
The identical days of summer
have been broken at last.
It is fall,
lustrous season that owns the future,
that has next year bunched up
in the clusters of tough red and white berries.
The light keeps ascending
the grassy slope past the shore.
Soon it will pass the border
of my body and the picnic table.
Soon it will reach past
the stands of sweet cedar and birch and pine.
Soon it will arrive at the maples,
and then, everything will be red.

IV

Diary

THE DAY'S CHORES: A LIST

1. A pale blue cup
   with tea in it,
   melted-down flowers
   first thing in the morning
   after one brown eye opens,
   and then the other,
   shining
   like the night they came from.

2. Then water the plants,
   there is no cat
   and it's good
   to have something
   purr with pleasure.

3. Has the sun been observed?
   Observe the sun.

4. There is work to do.
   How often I'm lazy!
   The back of my dreams has been broken,
   but work is still waiting.
   Now that I understand
   who it is, I try not
   to keep a lover waiting.

5. Sitting can be important,
   and a chair old enough
   to creak when I move.
   Let the chair speak,
   it belonged to an old man
   who never learned English.

6. Listen to someone else speak —
   it can be in a book

(especially if the person
assures you he was sad
the night not one star sang out.)

7. But ride the city bus too,
    once in daylight
    and again at night.
    That's where, yesterday, the old woman
    wondered if I was Jewish.
    She had a hurt, she said,
    I could tell you *things*, she said,
    I hate to say how that girl —
    and she was a *nurse* — how that one, she
    just after being so nice
    as you'd ever want to think
    while her mother-in-law was *alive*,
    she goes in there and *takes* them old
    them beautiful old wine glasses.
    And probate and everything and I
    didn't touch a thing.
    Right out of the house. Out
    of my sister's house. I tell you
    and it hurts, you know
    what I mean?

8. Also the grocery store,
    full of people
    flinging decision after decision
    into their metal baskets.
    On each of my fingers
    I write a word, a necessity
    of life: fish, spinach,
    flour, butter, milk,
    the brown mushrooms

38

whose sombreros I inspect
carefully.
One finger is sweet,
it is sugar,
it has a dream of sucking.

9. At home there is laundry,
    the vacuum cleaner,
    a cloth to rub a desk with,
    garbage piled up,
    music stacked and waiting
    in a brown envelope.
    Yesterday's mail looks old,
    it will never be answered.
    A wizened orange in a bowl,
    a slump in the afternoon
    when the sun is bright and blank
    just before the reentry of shadows.

10. A nap. But not long.
    Just enough
    for a second morning
    to pull from beneath the eyelids.

11. Candles, food, love with the one
    I light candles with.
    A record of the day,
    a precise diary
    rising fat or slivered
    every night over my shoulder.
    Something accomplished,
    a set of filed cards,
    white and remembered.
    This list is not tattered,
    no crossed-off thoughts.

39

12. I want to live,
        the first task is always
        before me. I call it
        groceries, laundry,
        poem, paint kitchen table,
        ask Stephen to explain relativity theory,
        call mother, fix bicycle;
        I say: go swimming, don't eat lunch
        today, read Bible this week, answer letters,
        find left purple mitten, ask
        landlady if kitten possible. . . .

        All these index cards
        and no index.
        I paint the table,
        I peel the orange,
        the sun has been observed
        personally by me today,
        something round
        and orange
        perfectly held
        wedge by wedge
        is in this day.
        I toss the orange up
        and catch it
        as I watch the setting sun.
        Something glistening, sweet
        with prisms is in my hand.
        I have a sense of the sun,
        his heart.

FOR KATHLEEN

Like a cake to cut through
you give us your madness,
sweet, white, a blizzard of words
that melts on your outstretched tongue.
Today your letter, how the people
at the Art Institute said, "Oh no!" They moved
away, your bits of paper fell from the table.
"I'm a crazy," you say.
You have a white angel, you need a bottle
to stuff him in, a bottle for your message.
You want something simple.
You told me you tried to be as ephemeral
as the Chinese poets, sending poems away forever
downriver on a peach blossom.
But here, Chicago, it's not like that.
You sailed your white message down
the Art Institute lunchroom.
How the ducks flew up with fear!
If someone were downstream,
if a willow bent agelessly over the water,
if we could touch a stranger's head,
knock gently from our own white room,
say, Home, home, anyone home?

GIRL AT A LIBRARY TABLE

Winter and the girl bends
over her book in the half-light.
She comes every day.
The librarian watches,
he loves her, the way she turns
the glossy pages with such tenderness.
She comes in the afternoon
as if for tea, for the sense of a drawing room,
a place with furniture and silk,
a salt white statue of Linnaeus the boy
twirling a flower in his hand,
claw feet on a mahogany table.
The heaviness of furniture, the privacy
of a public room. She comes
like a derelict warming her hands
at the flame of his books.
He has so much to give her!
He watches the red sun set behind her,
an apple of color with its white flesh secret,
shining, sinking away from him in the late afternoon.
He hands her coffee,
Vienna, a passion for Mozart,
anything, anything,
a pearl knife to slice through the pages,
the future.

MILK

It is October;
the leaves are yellow and falling
through the hazy, moist air.
I am falling, slumberously
through my own thick haze.
But last night at the crazy poetry society
a woman who looked like Marianne Moore
jabbed a finger at me, said
"Anybody can put down feelings —
but can you manipulate form?"

It's time to confess
I've never written a sonnet,
someone else thinks about internal rhyme schemes,
villanelles must be convent schools
where the daughters of the rich are trained
in etiquette.
The leaves are swirling
off the car as I drive to work.
I turn the corner,
a man who looks like Kissinger steps out;
he gets in a milk truck.
I want Kissinger to get in a milk truck
and drive away.

He will drive through the streets of our country
delivering milk to the children.
He'll visit with the housewives.
He'll tip his white cap and joke with the teenage boys.
He will prowl the grocery stores with Ginsberg,
visiting the dairy case at night.
He will learn a lot.

He will see the children going to school
and realize the small foreign power they are.

With their miniature lunch pails and scaled-down clothes,
they look like us.
He gives them cartons of milk.
He sees the women waiting on the corner for the bus.
They are going to sit at desks all day,
they are sad.
Give them milk, they need milk.

Pour milk down the throats of bankers,
the ones who raise the interest rates
(has your interest ever been aroused by a banker?)
Pour it in great gushes over weeping Chile,
over the bloody generals, down the long scar
that streaks the face of South America,
pour it over the sweet earth of Pablo's grave.

And K — you must make a stop
at the house of the lady who can write sonnets.
She is very old, she is afraid.
She has her tin cup in her hand, waiting.
You must fill it carefully with milk,
giving her time to learn how to drink.

You are in your truck early,
catching the rising, burning fog
of autumn, seeing the early morning leaves.
You find a shady street.
At first, it's too much for you:
all the emotion, the secrets of
the housewives and children,
the bankers and poets. The dead
and the warriors keep whispering
in your exhausted ear.
You go into the refrigerated van,
open the half gallons of milk,

44

and drink and drink, your head flung back.
First, the whole milk goes,
then the timid skim milk
that has nothing to say.
You drink the whipping cream,
the cream for morning coffee.
You gulp down the buttermilk,
that alien taste.
You're gnawing on cold sticks of sweet butter.
K — don't be afraid. We are the family of men and women.

Old women invite you in for breakfast.
Wherever you go, there is milk.
People call you The Milk Man.
K — close up the attaché case full of the lies
you must memorize tonight.
The spinsters are here,
they have an appointment to brief you about loneliness.
They have been drinking milk bravely alone for years.

Bow your head.
Let the poor
wash your head with milk.
This is a milk bath,
this is swimming in emotion.
Think of your mother if it makes you feel better.
Think of the poor: you cry.
Think of your life: you are shrieking.
Take the tin cup the committee of spinsters has ready.
Out on the streets you go from door to door,
the blind man you are, begging for milk.
The people are generous —
there is always milk for one more.

AT THE PARK

Two women pedal up on bikes.
One has a jaunty man's cap,
she is boyish and proud
to be with her friend.
She grins at me.
The other one is shy,
she is happy too,
but she only wants her friend
and the shore birds now.
No sign to me.
She takes a step, the ducks
whir off the grass
into the water.
The gulls are white,
they swoop with anticipation
for the plastic bag of bread crusts.
The two women throw bread
on the water,
they stomp on one old crust
to break it up.
They fling the white bread
confidently, far out on the water
as if this were a ball
in a man's game
they know how to play.
They would like to feed
the ducks, but ducks are shy.
Gulls are scavengers,
they are beautiful as they beg.
So little fear, the grace
of bread hurled, caught
in a lacquered beak
out of the blue air.
One woman cries out, "He took it

46

right in the air!"
I am peeling the twig
I picked up.
I want it perfectly naked,
sleek under the bark skin.
The gulls dip for the bread,
there is nothing
they would not do
for these women.
I peel the twig,
it is white and dry,
shining under its cocoon.
Perfect now, just its body,
white, smooth.
The ducks begin to think
they can risk coming nearer.
But it is too late, the bread
is all gone, gullward.
Now the gulls swoop
for joy alone, white crisps
against the sky, no bread,
just women, three faces.
I drop my peeled twig.
Three women watch
the ducks who are too shy, too late,
the gulls hurling their brightness
against the air, the morning sun.
Three women, empty-handed,
no words, very little naked flesh,
all this longing,
the white tokens flung out,
our way of swooping,
riding against the sun.

ON THE PORCH

Tonight voices come up
with the rain smell, the earth smell.
Through the open window
voices with their hieroglyphs of privacy;
not language, not exchanges
of love or good night, nothing overheard
that was meant to be secret,
just the voice, human and familiar
as the earth is the earth
with its old message soaking
into its skin.

THE COOKBOOK POEM

The writers of cookbooks come out at night,
the phantom cooks and their phantom recipes:
"Think about food, listen to us."
The no-nonsense compendium,
reeling with utensils,
with too many ideas about hamburger,
knowing everything there is to know
about how not to curdle, handing out
lists of government regulations
on butterfat content, diagrams
of cows, pigs, and sheep.

Then the gourmet cookbook
written by the fat man who says,
"Eating is a way of life."
The lists of unnatural unions
between chicken breasts and chocolate;
reasons why, ultimately, sirloin is more
economical than pot roast;
why every efficiency apartment should have
a copper salmon poacher.

The New England spinster who can tell
at three yards when you're going to die
has also written a cookbook:
the lady who says both Kennedy and Oswald
were "sanpaku," the whites of their eyes
showing between the iris and the lower lid.
And think of the public officials with B vitamin deficiencies,
the mashed potatoes and gravy consumed at state dinners,
the teenagers who, unnoticed by their mothers,
are gradually beginning to walk with their toes pointed
outward, victims of poor vitamin D assimilation.

Envy the lucky British!
All those teeth with all those open spaces
just because they had enough cod liver oil.
And the meat-eaters!
The eaters of muscle,
the silly old muscle-eaters —
there's scorn in that laugh.
"If you eat meat,
let it be liver."

These are the people who say
any child given brewer's yeast
at an early age in a natural
simple manner, will grow
to love it and will have no tolerance
for Hershey bars and Coca-Cola.
These are the anti-whipped cream people,
the no pie, no cake group,
the people who hate the fat man.
They are serious,
they are going to live longer than us.

The Quaker ladies have a cookbook too,
embarrassed and full of casseroles.
Recipes from Mabel Lockyer and Jeanette Coote,
Brazil Nut Sensation from Evelyn Dane
to go with Avocado-Chicken Surprise.
The moral cookbook with paragraphs
from A. J. Muste set between
Baked Chicken with Orange Rind
and Helen's Baked Lima Beans.

Literary cookbooks
with meals constructed

from scenes in *War and Peace* (Borodino Borscht)
and *A Farewell to Arms.*
The recipes by famous people:
Stravinsky Stew, an asparagus souffle
Jacqueline Kennedy Onassis enjoys
when dieting.
Authentic recipes from countries
that eat dumplings regularly,
places whose sole interest lies in their kolatches,
paella, Buddha's Delight.
Earnest books that tell you not to be afraid
to sprout your own beans,
nervous books that never begin a recipe without
telling you to wash something.
Books against unbleached flour, books for.
Books that think you're dumb: "Take an egg,
break it."
Books that say coriander and vanilla bean are staples.
Books that bicker at each other,
at their positions on butter and oleomargarine.

If you read long enough
the books themselves disappear.
Just the food remains, brilliant
as yarn samples.
The harmony is amazing —
you see wheat germ and whipped cream
meeting on frozen desserts;
mortars for mashing garlic;
apricot tarts, carrots and roast beef
together
as if they were meant to be that way.

They pass majestically by;
your eyes bulge.
Listen! It's not the food,
this is like traveling on the Continent.
Suddenly you're humble;
you want to memorize all the recipes for mayonnaise
    you can find.
You want to do everything they tell you,
never leaving out an herb or
deriding instructions to chop finely.
You make rash promises to bake bread
every week, to make your plates picture pretty,
to balance nutrients, color, texture, to grow
your own parsley.
You realize what a fool you've been.

It's hard to sleep on these nights,
after reading the cookbooks.
Ambition almost chokes you,
desserts especially.
You fall asleep,
wanting to be perfect.

ASCETICISM

1

The food we give each other
should be clear,
empty as wine glasses,
nonchalant like dirt.

The buoyancy we want
isn't at tables;
a worm ekes out a living
in the crevices of sidewalks.

After the rain it waits
sometimes in one body,
sometimes in two or three bodies,
to be useful

is lifted up
to nests where it is eaten.

2

St. Rose wore
white kid gloves once
and God gave her eczema
just to show her.

Sleeping on broken bricks
Rose of Lima tried not to notice
her own saliva,
how she swallowed it.

3

When we eat
we are like
everyone else.

A TIME ALONE:
NOTES FROM THIS WEEKEND,
MEMORIES FROM RELIGION

Matins

A mansion taken over by "the spiritual life,"
nuns as silent attendants.
Our religion sent us, for the rite of passage,
to the house gleaming like a laser
from the brain of the industrialist
who knew which immigrants to import
to build his railroad.
There, Jacobean flowers twirling
down the wallpaper, we were silent,
saw how the rich make winter warm them
in their globed, yellow sun porch.
A round room,
the expense of curved glass,
the ability to buy all directions,
to own the center.
We were there three silent days
held in a womb of money
deep inside the filmy sac
of our ancient, still-breathing religion.

and Lauds

Now,
yanked out 10 years from that
European double womb,
I've bought my way to silence again
with my own earned money.
I'm alone in a strange town.
I curl on the harsh bed known
to salesmen who break
my heart in the restaurant
with their jokes.

Prime

As if the LaCrosse *Herald*
were covering the serial
of my terrors, today's headline reads
2 MORE AREA WOMEN ASSAULTED:
the day I arrive, the rapist begins his work.
There is no retreat director here.
I take my clues from the papers
I buy in the motel lobby.
I pursue my terrors.
I am pursued.

Tierce

The boredom,
the sudden discovery
that boredom is terror.
Sinking through the color wheel
to find gray is next to orange.

Sext

The message is
no color today.
Paint your body
if you're lonely, actress.

Nones

The wine works.
I am filled with haze.

Vespers

The landscape of our nation has shrunk.
We find beauty in mosquito traps now.
I turn my chair to the motel window,
pallid end-of-the-world woman,
clutching Audubon's biographies of birds.
I hold his picture of the carrier pigeon up
to the white faces of the common birds that streak by.
Once Greece was green, a vegetable nation;
now it's loved for whiteness, the idea of something vacant.
Now we are doing that: in spite of myself,
I find beauty in this empty place.
Some streak of knowledge comes by;
it leaves a fine powder, a salt of memory
on my stretched-out body.
The sunset is good-bye to birds,
welcome to the chalk of night.

Compline

Tender
you are tender now
Go out.

Red

PRELUDE

A voice like a wedge speaks to us,
speaks against our life,
its daily illumination
in chairs, tablecloths, intimacy.
It speaks against these daisies in the vase,
against you,
my love.
It is the voice I call my serpent,
knowing it better than I know you.
It is the voice
of the larger needled trees
that speaks to women,
those about to marry.

LUNCH WITH THE IMPRESARIO

She stood on a bridge,
or maybe it was a restaurant
called The Bridge.
She was much younger than he.
Even though she wasn't his equal,
he spoke to her quite naturally.
"I could never make my hair glisten,"
she confided to him, and he nodded.
Even her black mustache,
which was a cat's,
was invisible, her face
was a watercolor.
"Precision," he said. "No precision."

Her face was a pastel smudge;
he was bald and definite.
The table where they sat
had a candle and a vase of carnations
which gave off the sharp clove smell of soap.
She told him the most important thing
that had ever happened to her
was the time her father said,
Don't let me *ever* catch you . . .
"There's truth in that," the man said.

He liked her; he said she had possibility.
But he decided on the geisha girl instead,
the one who moved like a moth.
"She's just perfect," he said.
He licked his thumb and forefinger,
and squeezed out the candle's flame.
Glistening hair and mustaches
just weren't in his line,

but he offered to buy her a Coke.
She left with her briefcase,
which was not graceful, but she had
so much to carry. He smiled and waved.
You'll make your way, he called after her,
I'm sure of that.

PISCES

I've spent the whole day reading
a girlhood book full
of governess dreams, governess stars,
the intense struggle
of the Victorian body for its mate,
their place clasped together on the burning bed.
Marriage on the bed, two gold fishes swimming,
one up, one down.
They must not snap their life cord;
like the fish in the horoscope
they must stay together, unbroken.
The love knot must not break,
must not splash red, red streak
over this gray March watery day.

Darling, says my aunt, red
is your color. And she buys me
a red coat that lasts forever,
and makes me hate it forever,
hate red, the human color,
the furthest color from fish.
Red, you shock me every month with your visit;
you have promised never to leave me
until I am old.
A tiny dot of red on the forehead of a woman
means something: she is married
or not married, something bloody or bloodless.

POEM FOR HIS WIFE

Her pure house stands around her,
waiting like a beast
for its husband.
Such a white tablecloth and new bread
breathing for dinner.

She puts her hands before her,
they are clean and steady
like hanging cages.

FIRE ENGINE

The women are singing.
At night the fireman lies awake sweating
with desire and terror.
The engines rise from the fog.
This is burning, this is drowning.
He makes a fist, promises something
to the white sheet.
The women are coming, riding
red horses, they swim in the air,
their drowning is for men,
their salt water comes in sharp flames.
He is no sword-swallower,
he drowns every night.
As they sing, the women's skirts flare with blood.
He is afraid of sirens, he says.
Women! he says, stuffing his ears with cotton.
See, it's a joke, he says.
He laughs,
but like a belly whose man has disappeared.

PIANO

Today, walking, we saw
the girl in the music store window,
her body bending
over the keyboard.
She sliced the air with the blades
of her long black hair;
the dahlias on the piano
were yellow as canaries,
their petals fell in a circle as she played.
We didn't speak,
for once we made no resolutions about listening.
The wide window held up its demonstration of silence.
Somewhere inside there was music,
but you and I stood on the sidewalk,
our hands unclenched and natural,
watching the thin fingers
rise and fall with their pink moons
over the black and white keyboard.
You pressed your lips to mine,
and the vibration, the music, glistened like milk.

MUSHROOMS

We hiked up the mountain that fall,
your father, you, and I.
Mushrooms were sprouting after the warm rain
from the black, leafy ground;
wet mushrooms, erect on their flesh-stems.

Like a tongue with its wheel of intelligence
flicking through the dark,
through a pastel body, a pine forest,
these newly lit flames struck out of the dampness;
tongues of fire speaking with the voices
of animals in the kingdom of wet leaves.

I called to you,
but you had climbed ahead;
your father, with his destination,
was leading you forward.
I stopped there alone.
On my knees
I stroked what rose
like a shivering stalk
from the red, red leaves.

FLOWERS IN A WATERFORD DECANTER

The two irises you gave me today
glide out of the cut glass decanter
you also gave me.
Two gifts with two years
between their giving.
Behind your gift comes
your attempt at serenity,
the life we talk of given form,
attaching itself silently
to a small object
the way a modern wife tries to cling
gracefully, as if with necessity
to a husband.

Prisms shoot out from the glass;
the yellow-lipped irises,
long stemmed and natural, rise
from the glass garden,
from your idea of beauty,
the beauty I love too.
They rise like swans palely lighted,
lavender and down-throated;
their petals bow softly.

We are silent, reading.
I see you look up too
from your book to lose
yourself in the loveliness
you've brought home.
Love, now, this moment,
let us admit
we need this loneliness,
the moment our faces meet
nodding, like someone drowsy,
over the deep blossom.

FLOWERS IN A LIFE

1

Always back to the flowers,
they were the earliest thing.
My father in his greenhouse
for 40 years surrendering
season after season to roses.

2

The Austrian growers were muddy
as roots, they chewed tobacco
and spat on the ground.
I spit and they laughed.
My clear spit settled
like a drop of thick water
on the ground. Their spit
was brown and flecked
with sharpness.
So many years in the mines of horticulture,
so much swallowed earth.
I thought: when I grow up
I will spit dirt too.

3

Don't call it dirt,
the old grower said
when I played at his potting table,
This is earth, this here.

4

Rosebuds on a plate.
Flowers never seemed feminine before:
only men in the greenhouses, surrounded

68

by a million pink blossoms.
But I was surrounded by flowers,
a small honorary male
in a man's world.
I could watch for hours.

5

I had assumed flowers had blood
in their veins,
but even I understood
the orchid is a bloodless creature.
Nothing will ever be so white again,
their coolness, the damp heat of their mansions.
I noticed this too: only the rich
asked to see the orchid house.

6

The florist must be a businessman
in the midst of flying pollen,
odor, a desire for sleep.
He knows money
does not fade
like the flower.

7

I found lilacs on my own,
coming home from school,
like everyone else.
The national flower
with a private odor. Dying,
we will each one day see the lilac
flare up with its flask of stars.

8

At the center of the anemone
loveliness stops, it disappears,
tightens, blackens, bristles,
balls itself into a furry mound
of privacy.
Does every woman want
to be beautiful? Not beautiful,
but a flower, the black knob
of furry sex finally exposed
through the damp petals
of red, of purple, white,
through the thrilling amber,
to the black cat of privacy.

9

You
as a flower.
You and myself
who am something reaching too.
If I could hold up one thing
to show you what I mean
about myself lately,
it would be this yanked-out Swedish ivy,
potted in pure air
no water
no earth
and yet, not dying either.

But I wanted to show you
yourself
for once:
the flower has no name;

70

it has long life, its father
was a tree in Colorado,
the blossom itself must be yellow
and shivers like a wind-bell.
It cannot remember its roots
but they are knotted like a tree's and heavy.
It has the odor of dirt like a new mushroom.
Like the moss rose, it opens its bright face
to the sun early and is alone in joy.

We have loved flowers
and poems about flowers.
You told your mother
to plant a lilac over your grandmother's grave
because it is the poet's flower.
You read me the old man's poem about the asphodel
to make me love you again.
So, if I call you a flower
this one time
I have reason.
I have always been accurate
in my heart
where your name,
that gold wand,
has swept the air
before me so long.
I love you
I love the yellow rose.
I am at home with flowers
and will begin this life,
like every other one,
with a blossom held out
to a flaming mountain.

 **VI**

Mystical Cities

Is it lack of imagination that makes us come
to imagined places, not just stay at home?
Or could Pascal have been not entirely right
about just sitting quietly in one's room?

Continent, city, country, society:
the choice is never wide and never free.
And here, or there. . . . No. Should we have stayed at home,
Wherever that may be?
      — Elizabeth Bishop, "Questions of Travel"

GALENA, THE FUTURE

for Timothy and Theresa

We said we'd go back to live,
and we carried the old red hotel with us when we left.
A red-haired girl rode by on a horse
and you said, "It's the 19th century!"

The town is on the Mississippi in Illinois.
My mother understood our excitement:
"Yes, your great-grandfather started West
from Galena in a covered wagon . . ."

Since that visit four years ago
I've wanted to know
if this could be the place
where all of us could live,
my mother,
my brother who read my diary and laughed,
me,
some future child and his pet, a large dog?

Or is it as you said
(and you were happy about it)
the 19th century,
a town pressed like a peony blossom
in a family album,
surrounded by pictures
of our sturdy dead,
their blood having run into my blood
to survive somehow; they wanted to survive.

Everyone I love is looking for a new way to live,
but it is our mothers we rescue
in forsaken river towns,
with small vegetable gardens and baked bread.

The red-haired girl, breathless,
rides the dramatic horse.

A woman, my grandmother now dead, is baking bread.
Her daughter remembers
a flowered mixing bowl, now cracked,
the dough rising gently, changing as slowly as time.
Does she lift the damp linen towel? Does she peek?
Does her mother let her touch, but lightly, gently,
the warm pulse of the sunny round?
"This is a live thing, like a plant, a growing shoot . . ."
The child who would be a widow says to herself,
". . . a flower growing inside. . . ."

Those two loved each other.
The younger was sad when the other died
and the old woman said, even to the priest
she admitted, no, she did not want to leave.
She went, recognizing no one,
remembering whatever she remembered.
It was she who took the 19th century,
she who didn't mean to take it.

To survive
we must go forward, just as the family dead
know they must surge into us, their future.
It is not enough to recognize the beauty of perfect moments,
to use them like full red roses in heavy glass to weight our lives.
No,
allow beauty to stop

allow the beautiful body which has been our motto
to go unclothed
so it may disintegrate
and form the strict pulsing geometric movements
it has wanted for so long,
let it out into the black intense depth field
where it will discharge itself of every impulse,
or maybe, lie still, a silent huddle of lines indicating . . .
                                    but in the future.

ST. PAUL: WALKING

The old city of saints opens its hand again this morning,
    its claw of money and glass rosaries.
I never say no.
Together we have broken bread, promises, hearts,
    whatever drags beneath our muddy river.
I put my bare hand on the red stone of the millionaire's house:
    it sizzled like water in a black pan.
Sometimes I think I will hold forever the hand of this city;
    it shakes its fist of beer and greenhouses at me,
      its long death sways on the stem of an orchid even in winter.

NOTES FOR TSVETAYEVA

A Bonnard head, but not in a garden; round,
simple, one ringing globe in the city
of forty times forty golden church towers.
I dreamed that same dream:
you have your singing sisters,
they wear Chinese silk,
their weedy skirts are marbled
like endpapers in a rare book on birds.
They swirl because this is underwater.
We sing in water.

Doors open. Tsvetayeva floats in. She sleeps
by drowning. The water rises slowly around her,
stillness over the ripple of insomnia.
I hold her hand.
I fall this way too at night.

The seven hills of Moscow, the seven of St. Paul.
We string the beads of our blood on a length
of old streetlights as we walk our native cities at night.
We love our cities.
There are praying nuns and people too rich
with stone houses; orchids at Christmas in a pink box;
a brewery where a worker burns to death;
parks where no one sits in winter, and the snow-crusts
cheapen and darken like a burnt meringue.
Old men sit in libraries to keep warm.
The silence of a city in a country in the heart of its winter.

Our other shared city, Prague;
more hills, more churches, more beer, the golden light
of churches and beer, the same cut lemon
of a round streetlight, the dark clothes
of people who carry lilacs to work in waxed paper.
Tsvetayeva says a terrible good-bye in Prague,

separation on the Charles Bridge.
Male tears like a river rising, fish swim
in her eyes. Male tears mean the end,
no boat keeps afloat on those salt waters.
Sister! The saints surround you!
The saints and something ordinary,
wilting lilacs someone has placed in a jar.
If only I were there, could tell you . . .
But this is before I was born.
Your hand goes to your face, so much
water, so few boats.

DREAM AFTER TRAVEL: PRAGUE

for Marly Rusoff

You, with a pile of shawls,
    the one for me is weed-green
    wool challis the color of lichen,
    silvery, fringed, spread like a cloth
    in a forest of blue needles.
Another baroque pastel from that city,
    the color of an old bulding afloat, face up, in the Vltava,
    someone's drowning from a top window,
    a row of pink geraniums on the sill.
    The blood of someone dead fills my eyes.

Your hand is white, capable, a grandmother's
    hand that has already grasped
        so much work
    but young, thin-boned.
At last you free the shawl, we see
    it was caught in a pile of long bright aprons:
    it is the only shawl.
I want to hold your hand as it shakes the cloth.
You wear a Bohemian garnet on your finger,
it is square,
    a dark clot above the knuckle-bone,
it belonged to an immigrant from that pale gold city.

Suddenly the stone becomes huge,
as big as a window, each rosy facet makes
a separate pane of glass; a great set of garnet
    French windows with gold knobs
    opening onto the balcony.
Here, you say, politics has always been a matter
    of jumping out of windows . . .
and that begins our old argument all over again.

But we put our faces to the glass, biting
     the lip of blood which forms a language,
     the silence which is Slavic and only partly ours.

Inside this wine window we spread out the aprons,
I toss the shawl on a black velvet chair;
a man comes in who deals in forged passports,
he drinks champagne and tells a risqué anecdote.
So many things are out of place:
     Just as they should be, you remind me.
I feel I am inside a color.
     Yes, yes, that's history, you say.

Something that was deep-colored has faded,
a country rooted like a tooth in Europe has been hollowed out
     and its gold is in a foreign pocket.

We stood for a moment in the garnet heart of that history,
     passing peasant curios between us, a Jew and a Gentile,
     tourists at a dusty Czech spa, drinking bitter water
          from a cup still passed back and forth
          among the children of this sad country.

ELEGY FOR THE BURNED

January 1969
Anthracite sours the air,
the sun's no better than a gas lamp,
and the cocaine of the fog
has confused the trees.
Later, slush chokes the gutters;
the moon will elude
the oily clouds as it rises
over the russet tiles
of the fluted roofs.
Icicles are dangling
from the eaves of the Czernin Palace
where Jan Masaryk
jumped, or was pushed,
but definitely died,
twenty-one years ago.
On Vaclavske Namesti
Jan Palach has lit his match.
He has breathed his last gold
in the golden city,
he has become many colors.
In the emergency room
of Bellevue Hospital
my brother fights to save
the melting bodies
of two other men
who tried to go up in smoke
in front of the U.N. building.
It's the fingernails, he says.
You can't get the fingernails
out of their gums.
They double over,

they crouch down and dig
into their mouths
one last time, but
the right words
aren't there anymore.

   May 1977
We sit around a white
linen cloth stitched with red
geometric embroidery.
A tall bottle of *slivovice*
on the table, flecks
of caraway in the bread,
a mound of codfish roe heaped
like tiny greased ball bearings.
Outside, the engaged couples
move in and out
of the Persian lilacs.
One man, a doctor, tells us
there was never any hope,
then or now.
Later, we raise our glasses
in the high-ceilinged apartment.
Drink fast! they say. Don't think!
We throw back our heads.
Our tongues burn briefly,
then our throats.
It is gone, the colorless
abstract of blue plums,
the heat distilled
in dusty Moravian towns,
the forgotten villages,

84

the narrow highways
lined with fruit trees
that very soon will
rush into flower,
all those flimsy pink blossoms.

TO A CZECH EXILE

Prague does not let go,
either of you or of me,
chère Patricia.

On the windowsill, wild asters and three stalks of harebell
in a plastic glass. Then the window itself,
the shoreline of stones, the big lake, the gilt slit
of the horizon where water careens into sky.
Nothing but America for eighty more miles, Luboš;
then Canada takes over.
Superior is the world's largest freshwater lake.
I want you to know that,
I'm American, I love statistics.
In Toronto you walk around the streets,
you want to ask strangers, *What is this "freedom?"*
But nobody thinks it's there anyway.
It's impossible to understand how I feel, you say.
Impossible how those same gold sunsets keep
tightening behind your eyelids
every single day.

Ten years ago you and Jan stood on the Charles Bridge.
You made those wild statements about art and freedom.
You walked together in the Kampa. It was May.
The horse chestnuts were in flower, the blossoms
looked like cheap paper someone had shredded
into a million pink bits.
The arrow of your country
was "the heart of Europe" again.
You were where you belonged,
the center of history,
home,
"the most beautiful city in Europe,"
the loveliest bridge in the world,
the oldest university in Central Europe —
I can't help these statistics, Luboš.

It's only now we say to each other
how ironic it was that you were studying
pantomime that whole year:
the silent art of a small nation
that keeps its lip buttoned.
Even in the Kampa it didn't occur to you
the horse chestnuts were clairvoyant,
and so much would be torn to bits.
You don't like to look at things that way,
but you do it all the time now.

You're reading *Labyrinth of the World,
Paradise of the Heart* by Comenius.
You say you disagree with him,
the part about paradise being in the heart.
Of course, you say, no point
in crying one's heart out. No point
to crying, no point to streetlights
that won't stop burning in your eyes,
no point to bridges or baroque palaces,
to Kafka's fear of his father,
his city of warehouses and saints, no point
on the compass, just
the steely point of memory,
the sharp stick that writes over and over,
I miss Prague so *terribly badly*.

SCIENCE FICTION
AT A SAN FRANCISCO BEACH

This beam (part of a smashed ship?) is my chair,
lying where the sea put it, softened and crumbling
like moist humus from its salt life, salt settled in its fiber,
making from impenetrable solid a link to another state,
something almost ready to slip into new life, new use. A compost.

We are like that. Almost ready.
Almost earth from old solid chunks.
Is it necessary to dissolve?
Are these promises —
that our body and its mind will merge,
will find so much beauty in perception
that salt and sand, salt and foam will sweep into the channels of
      the heart,
down the smallest territories of blood and bone,
to change us,
and we, humans, we will hear and see.
Hear not the ocean but the ocean's ocean
as if it were inside that blue, fluted shell itself,
sounding with the sound.
And to see — to see we will close our eyes.

But how long has this crumbling beam rested on the shore?
How many changes has it felt through its fiber?
And still it serves for a chair, is solid enough, still
has more time to put in, waiting.

It is miraculous that living in a decaying city (I've been here two
months and the newspaper, morning and evening, has at least one
headline describing it that way, and a story to tell why) that in this
decaying city, you can get on a streetcar, ride to the end of the line
and be . . . here. Ocean. Something you'd thought was gone, not
yours anymore, not ours. Here is: sand, a long beach of sand, col-
ored almost black from wetness, then getting pale, paler, very pale,
until the white-beige of the dunes holds it great drabness against

the city we can't see. Also hills, empty except for a slim branch of pastel houses that might be Genoa, and sky and the water itself crashing and foaming with its family of birds, its shells and fragments washed up, damped out, like this beam that still, in a very high tide, becomes a marine creature.

Who can say how much we need this place? On Market Street I saw a man look at me, through me, in an agony of release and torment as he peed, swaying against a mailbox. "Can't get it up any other way," the bum on the corner, his friend, explained as I passed.

We walk sleeping but dreamless, fretting constantly.
Living this way, when we close our eyes
we see nothing, or maybe some of us,
a slight gold light
that fails instantly.
Glitter,
we say glitter and distrust it.
So many chances are lost.
Salt and sand run through an hourglass
then, turned, run through again and
turned and again . . .

An old man (he is lonely) comes up. "Hello. I don't want to interrupt . . . I see you're writing . . ." (smile, is it all right to smile?) "Well, I did want to finish this . . ." (no, you have to move on). . . . "Well, I'll be here tomorrow. Tomorrow maybe you'll be here. Maybe I'll see you tomorrow."

Each tomorrow, three tomorrows settled in their simple declarative shells he laid down, gave me as easily as I might have given — what? A smile? He is a tiny grain, far away along the beach now. His old black coat is a round grain far away. He was important. He was here, making promises about the future:

> *Tomorrow let's go to the beach*
> *I'll see you tomorrow*
> *Tomorrow is the first day of Spring*

But last night I dreamed about the end of the world,
and it was very real and not far away. It was here.
The monstrous sights, the screaming!
Then, silence for a long, long time.
I woke up, crying out of loyalty for what we are,
this ugliness of our allegiance.
Because as my friend said
(my friend who speaks quite plainly with the spirits of the dead),
There is so much evil
but none of us knows an evil person.

We are missing something and mean to find it
so we can be ourselves. Maybe for the first time.
I know almost nothing,
but it looks as if it is altogether in the future.
Yet it is the details, always the details, we must watch:
　　grains of colored sand (if you look, it is colored);
　　the common chalky shells that lie broken on the beach —
　　occasionally you find a whole one, emptied of its
　　creature, but imprinted with its body to prove this animal
　　took the shape of an opened flower;
　　or an old man, barefoot with his shoes laced together, slung
　　across his shoulder. He is walking on the beach. He may
　　ask for the time or a cigarette.

Don't worry about the love,
the love will come.
It will appear even as things turn their old-coated backs on you,
as living itself or your lover are taken away.
Slowly, breathing and pulsing in sea-rhythm,
the time will have been spent,

for to you who are decay who are humus who are flower
the details accumulate, like evolution, into a body,
a body swaying out of itself, out and out,
the wave of the body eluding the wires of the skin,
recognizing no boundaries.

We will not be uplifted.
This is not transfiguration, but disappearance.
A matter of the salt, after its slow process,
the dance of all these years,
finally reaching the softened golden pulp of the heart,
and the beam, after so long, falls
silently
lovingly
away from itself,
being neither one thing nor the other.

PITT POETRY SERIES

Paul Zimmer, General Editor